Follow the Leader

Follow
the Leader

THE STORY OF CONDUCTING

By ROBERT W. SURPLUS

Illustrated by GEORGE OVERLIE

Musical Books for Young People

LERNER PUBLICATIONS COMPANY

MINNEAPOLIS, MINNESOTA

To Amy and Melanie

International Copyright Secured. Printed in U.S.A.

Library of Congress Catalog Card Number: 62-20801

Published simultaneously in Canada
by The House of Grant

Second Printing 1963
Third Printing 1964
Fourth Printing 1966

CONTENTS

Concert Time

Concert time is eight-thirty. By eight o'clock, there is great activity around the concert hall. Outside, there are taxis bringing people to the concert, big cars stopping to let out important people, and men and women trying to buy tickets at the box-office at the last minute.

Inside, the ushers are showing people to their seats and handing them programs for the evening's concert. The musicians are coming on stage and are getting ready for their work. Some make a last check of their instruments, while others play special drills, or "warm-ups", which they find helpful in getting ready to play a concert. Some of the musicians practice parts from the music for the evening's concert.

Many of the people in the seats are reading their programs. The program lists the music that will be played and the names of the composers. A special section, called *program notes,* gives information about the music and tells about the lives of the composers.

About twenty minutes after eight, a man with a violin under his arm walks to the center of the stage. He stops right next to a small platform called a *podium.* This is the platform on which the conductor will stand when he directs the orchestra. The man with the violin under his arm is the *concertmaster,* or leader of the violin section. Next to the conductor, he is the most important person in the orchestra. In many orchestras, he serves as assistant conductor.

The concertmaster signals to the orchestra, and the musicians stop their "warm-ups". It is time for tuning the orchestra. The oboe sounds an A, and the players quickly tune their instruments. When their instruments are tuned, they sit quietly, waiting for the concert to begin.

A sudden burst of applause signals that the conductor is making his way to the podium. He bows to the audience in response to their applause, and then steps on the podium. He glances at the orchestra, and thinks silently about the *mood* of the music and the *tempo*, or speed, at which the first selection begins. He raises his *baton,* a thin wooden stick about twenty inches long. The concert is about to start. As his baton comes down, the musicians in the orchestra respond, and the sound of music fills the hall.

The musicians in a good orchestra are so highly skilled that they seem to play with no effort at all. Everything sounds so polished and goes so smoothly that it almost seems as though the orchestra could play without a conductor.

Is this so? Is a conductor really necessary? Why do we have conductors? Do they only wave a baton at concerts, or do they have other duties? What do they really do? Let's take a look at history and see if we can discover some of the answers to these questions.

6

Early Conductors

The first conductors date back to the time when the church was the center of musical life. The music of the early church was *chanted*. This means that the words were sung to very much the same rhythm as they were spoken. There were stopping or breathing places, the same as when people speak. The music was called *Gregorian chant*, after the name of a pope who collected and arranged the chants.

When choirs were started to sing this music, the singers faced several problems that they could not solve by themselves. In trying to find answers to these problems, they thought of the idea of having one person stand in front of the choir and *conduct,* or lead the music.

One reason why a conductor was needed was that people talk at different speeds. This sounds funny when we are talking about music and singing, but remember that chanting is like speaking. Some people talk fast, some slow. Some people begin a sentence quickly, and then slow down. Some people begin slowly, and then speed up. Others have a jerky, "start-and-stop" way of speaking. A choir is made up of many different kinds of people. If the chanting was to sound good, someone was needed to help the singers sing the words together.

As choirs grew larger, the singers quickly saw a second reason for having a conductor. It is easy for a small group of four to six singers to stay together when singing, but a group of ten to twenty finds it much harder. If a choir had more than a few members, a leader would be quite helpful in keeping the singers together.

The early choirs did not read music from books, since music was not written as it is today. Instead, little signs over the words, called *neumes* (newms), showed if the melody went up or down. Only the choir director had a copy of the words and neumes. The singers sang the music by heart, and watched the leader for signals to help them sing the right notes. A conductor was needed to show them just how the music went.

A fourth reason for having a conductor grew out of the use of divided choirs in churches. In this kind of chanting, one choir sang part of the music and was answered by a second choir. Another way was to have a leader sing the first part, and then to have the whole choir answer. Sometimes *Swing Low, Sweet Chariot* is sung this way today. This type of singing is called *antiphony* (an-TIF-o-nee). It is very much like a question and an answer. A good musician was needed to be the leader—someone who could understand the neumes and sing the music correctly.

Everyone sang the melody in this early church music. For this reason, the music was called *monophony* (mo-NAHF-o-nee), or "one-voice" music.

As time went on, composers wrote music with several melodies sung at the same time. Each of these melodies was a tune by itself, but they were all sung together to make a more interesting piece of music. Each part had different notes and a different rhythm from the other parts.

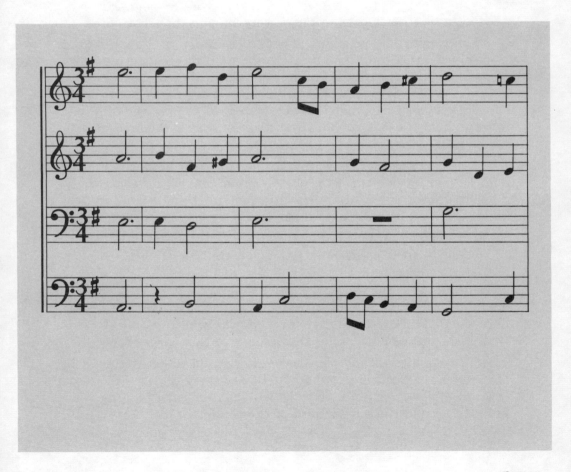

If you have played in a band or orchestra, or have sung in a choir, you know that having a different part from others makes it harder to stay on your own part. Maybe you can also remember when you sang rounds in school. Sometimes, you put your fingers in your ears, so you could be sure of staying on your own part.

This type of music with its many melodies was called *polyphony* (po-LIF-o-nee). It was much harder for singers to stay together than when everyone sang the same part. It was also much harder to hear all the parts at once. Now, more than ever, a conductor was needed to keep the singers together. Also, someone with a "good ear" was needed to be sure that the singers were singing the right notes.

So far, we've been talking about the conductors of choir music. Today, when we think about a conductor, our first thought is usually of the man who directs a symphony orchestra. The orchestra really got its start during the days of polyphony. When music began to be sung in several parts, instruments were used to play the different parts to help the singers. This was a step towards the orchestra as we know it.

The early orchestras were not like the great orchestras of today. In fact, at one time, they were called *accidental orchestras*. The conductor was never sure what instruments he would have, and it was "just an accident" if the group were *balanced* (each part equal in loudness). Have you ever played with a group like this?

Around 1600, something happened that was to change both orchestras and conducting. In the city of Florence, Italy, operas were being given for the first time. People were very interested in opera. It was a new kind of entertainment for them. Ask your parents about how popular television was when it first started. Opera was just as popular for the Italians of that earlier time.

The big interest in opera was very helpful to orchestras. The early opera orchestras soon had twenty to forty players. They sat in front of the stage, in a place called the *orchestra pit,* and were grouped around the harpsichord of the conductor.

10

Notice that we said the "harpsichord of the conductor". As time went on, there were several ways of conducting that were used. One of the most popular ways of conducting was from the harpsichord.

The man who sat at a harpsichord and conducted was called a *keyboard conductor*. By the beginning of the seventeenth century, the keyboard conductor was very much in style. He was a busy man. Let's see why.

In those days, composers did not write out all the parts as they do today. They wrote the melody, or tune, and the bass, or lowest part. Sometimes they wrote a few more parts, but often they gave only an outline. The conductor and the musicians had to make up music from a special part called *figured bass*.

Look at the example of figured bass shown below. The melody, or singer's part, is on the upper staff and is written in the treble clef. The bass part is found on the lower staff and is written in the bass clef. Notice the numbers under the bass part. These are the figures that told the musicians what notes to play.

EXAMPLE 1

This is how it was done. The musician looked at the bass part and called each bass note *one*. Then he saw what numbers were written below each note. Starting with one, he counted up the number of notes that the figures told him to count. He then played those notes as part of the music. Example two shows the easiest way this could be done. The numbers have been marked behind the notes of the first three chords. Can you tell how the rest of the notes in this example have been chosen?

EXAMPLE 2

Once the music was passed out and the instruments tuned, the conductor seated himself at the harpsichord and gave the signal to begin. Then the fun began!

The conductor had to play his own part on the harpsichord. Remember, this included making up a lot of the music as he went along. If a singer or player got lost, he had to play the missing part to help the lost musician find his place. If a singer or player got ahead or behind the orchestra, the conductor had to straighten him out with the harpsichord. If a singer changed tempo, or speed, the conductor had to see that the orchestra did, too. He was careful that the sound of the instruments did not drown out the singers. He also started the group, set the beginning tempo, and showed the beat all the way through the music. Everyone depended on this one man, who was busy enough playing the harpsichord to begin with.

On nights when things were going well and the orchestra and singers were right together, the conductor would make up a fancier part. Musicians of this time loved to show how they could invent music on the spot. Example three shows how a conductor might play from a figured bass part on such a night.

EXAMPLE 3

There are three *staves,* or lines of music. The upper one is the singer's part, while the music invented by the conductor can be found on the bottom two staves, or *grand staff.* Notice that all the notes in example two are found in example three. Instead of playing the notes all at once in a chord as in example two, the chords are broken apart, making a sound something like a harp. The same notes written differently can also be found in the middle line, or right hand of the harpsichord part.

Let's imagine a night when all sorts of things went wrong. The singer forgot the words and sang the wrong words about three notes behind the orchestra. Some of the violinists got careless and pulled ahead of the rest of the orchestra. In trying to straighten everyone out, the conductor played his part as in example four.

EXAMPLE 4

In the right hand, shown on the middle line, he played the melody to help the singer. To make the melody even stronger, he played it in octaves (the same melody eight notes lower in addition to the top part). In trying to get everyone together, he played strong "oom-pah" chords with his left hand to bring out the beat of the music.

Because the conductor was so busy, the concertmaster started to help out. He watched over the playing of the strings, and began to beat time by moving his violin up and down. Sometimes, he used his bow to beat time. Some concertmasters beat time by stamping with their feet on the floor. Even if some of them were a bit noisy, good concertmasters could help out a lot.

You've heard the old saying that "too many cooks can spoil the broth". Well, two or more conductors can spoil the music—especially if they don't agree.

Sometimes the conductor and concertmaster had different ideas about how fast the music should go. It was quite easy for this to happen at the beginning of a piece of music.

Suppose you were playing in an orchestra with two conductors who weren't really conductors, but players like yourself. You would have an idea about how fast the music should go, and so would all the other players. Some would follow one conductor, some the second conductor. Others wouldn't trust either conductor—they would figure they knew as well as anyone else how fast the music should go. It might take five or ten measures for everyone to start playing together. I'm sure you know how such a performance would sound.

The Germans had a funny name for this sort of thing. When an orchestra couldn't get together at the start of a piece of music, they said they were playing the "dog bars". They used this name, since they felt such music was not fit for human ears.

At other times, the concertmaster might play his part too loudly in trying to keep the group together. Maybe the conductor would get lost himself, and play the same chords over and over on the harpsichord. Maybe both men would *accent* (play louder) the first beat of a measure too much. There were lots of things that could go wrong when there was more than one conductor. The idea that "no man can serve two masters" was right as far as the musicians were concerned.

There were some conductors who did not direct from a keyboard instrument. This was true of many of the church choir directors, as well as some of the orchestra conductors. A conductor who didn't use an instrument used his hands, some kind of baton (buh-TAHN), or a roll of paper. Others stamped their feet or hit their music stands with a baton to give the beat of the music. Some choir directors even directed with a handkerchief tied on a stick!

The batons that were used were quite interesting. We have already mentioned that a roll of paper was used by some conductors. This custom may have come from the time when the Sistine Choir in Rome was conducted with a roll of paper called a *sol-fa*. Other batons were short sticks of wood. Still others were made of bone, ivory, or leather.

Some conductors used a long heavy piece of wood to beat the time. They pounded the floor to give the beat of the music and to keep the musicians together. This type of baton was so heavy that it made a lot of noise when it was used. Conductors who used this kind of baton were soon called "wood choppers".

Almost everyone was unhappy with the noise made by many conductors. Can you imagine what such noise could do to the choir's part in a church service? Do you think you could stand this pounding if you were listening to a concert? Many people asked for a baton that would give directions to just the *eyes,* and not the *ears,* too.

Have you ever heard of anyone being killed by a baton? Well, such a thing really happened, and a fine composer and conductor was lost.

Jean Baptiste Lully was the most powerful musician in all France. He had complete control of everything that took place in

music in the whole country. While he was a fine musician and a good organizer, he had several bad faults. One of his faults was his failure to control his temper. More than once he was said to have smashed a violin over the head of a musician. Bad temper or not, he was a good conductor for those days.

In the end, however, his temper proved to be his undoing. While conducting some of his own music, he grew so angry that he pounded the floor harder than usual. Somehow, his foot got in the way, and he accidentally pounded his own foot with his heavy baton. Blood poisoning started, and he died shortly after. Quite a baton, wasn't it?

The Rise of the Baton

Both the two-conductor system and keyboard conductors lasted a long time, even though music was changing. But little by little, the baton was winning out!

Vienna was amazed in 1812 when a conductor named Mosel used a baton. In 1817 concert-goers in the German cities of Dresden and Frankfurt were surprised to see orchestras led the same way. When the German conductor, Spohr, went to London, the directors of the London Philharmonic Society were very unhappy when he pulled a baton out of his pocket. They didn't want the orchestra to be led with such a thing! The players, however, were so pleased with this new kind of conducting that they clapped very loudly after they had played only one movement of the symphony. Other conductors, famous musicians such as von Weber and Mendelssohn, were also using batons.

There were a number of good reasons why conducting with a baton was becoming more popular. First, there was a big change in the orchestra. The modern orchestra got its start when composers stopped writing figured bass and began to write complete parts for every instrument. No longer did the musicians make up their own music. Every note was there for them to play—right down to the last dot!

While others had a hand in it, the composer Franz Joseph Haydn, is given much of the credit for starting the modern orchestra. When he stopped writing the *cembalo part* (chem-BAH-lo), another name for the harpsichord part, a number of things happened. Remember how the harpsichord was used to fill in the empty spaces between the melody and the bass part? Haydn had to find something else to fill in the missing notes, so he began to use the wind instruments for this. He also had them play the melody at times. Up to this time, wind instruments were not given much to do. Nobody really knew what to do with them until Haydn came along.

The new job given the winds meant that these instruments became more important. Soon, more wind players were used in the orchestra. Wind players get tired faster than string players, so composers gave them resting periods in the music. When it was time to play after one of these rests, they often needed help in starting. Today, when a conductor signals at such a spot, we say he is giving a *cue*. With the wind instruments making a lot of *entrances*, or coming in at different points in the music, it was a lot harder to keep the orchestra together.

When composers stopped writing figured bass and wrote out all the parts, they began to grow more fussy about how their music was to be played. In the days of figured bass, some of the players were not as careful as they might have been. Now, all that was changed—the composers wanted their music played exactly as they had written it. They even began to tell the players how loud or how soft to play. To do this, they wrote Italian words on the pages of music. These are called *dynamic markings* (die-NAM-ik), and are known to musicians all over the world.

Some of the really great composers wrote music for an orchestra that did not exist—that is, they wrote for more instruments than were used in the orchestra of their day. In this way, they forced the orchestra to become larger.

Conductors were growing more important for another reason. The common people were beginning to do things in music. In the past, music had been for just kings and nobles. Now, instead of just the nobility hearing good music, anyone who had enough money to get into a concert hall could attend concerts. Hearing good music made people want to play or sing, and many new musical organizations were started.

Composers had conducted their own music up until now. Suddenly, there were so many places for music to be played that composers could not conduct all these concerts. The *career-conductor* now took the place of the *composer-conductor*. Some composers were also conductors, but people no longer felt that the composer was the best one to conduct his own music. He might be, but he might not be. In fact, some people began to think that a composer was the poorest one to conduct his own music. This wasn't so, either. Some of the greatest composers were wonderful conductors —men like Handel, Bach, Berlioz, Verdi, Wagner, Mahler, Richard Strauss, and others.

Not everyone was convinced that the baton should be used. Some conductors still led the orchestra with their violins. The old style of having two conductors was still used when music for both orchestra and chorus was performed. In fact, when the Beethoven ninth symphony was first performed, there were three conductors —one a keyboard conductor, one a waving violinist, and Beethoven himself, who beat the time.

Some very good musicians didn't care for the baton at all. Robert Schumann, the famous composer, did not like it one bit that Mendelssohn used a baton to conduct. Musicians, who should have seen the reasons why a baton was needed, fought against its use. Some of them just didn't understand how much the orchestra and orchestra music had changed. Others just didn't like any change—they wanted to keep the old figured bass.

A musician called Fabian wrote a book poking fun at conductors. He said that any man who could beat time through a whole opera with his right hand, and still move that hand the next morning was a far better man than he was. He knew he didn't have that much strength, and that to do this a man would need arms stronger than a "thrasher", a person who harvested grain. What won't people think of when they are against something new!

The little white stick of wood was not concerned about any of this. It did its job when called upon, and it was called upon more often as time went on. During the nineteenth century, the war over what to use to conduct was over—the baton had won!

Getting Ready for a Concert

Program Planning

One of the conductor's many duties is the job of deciding what music the orchestra should play. The programs for an entire *season* are decided upon well in advance. The orchestra season begins in the fall and ends in late spring. The music that will be played on every program for the entire season is usually chosen by the end of August. Sometimes, when a conductor goes to Europe for the summer or to a summer job in another city, he will have his programs all planned before he leaves.

How does a conductor choose the music for his programs? What does he think about in making his choices? He has several good guides to help him in planning his concerts.

There are about two hundred pieces of music that are called the *standard repertoire* (reh-peh-TWAH). These are all favorites of audiences, and are by such famous composers as Beethoven, Brahms, Mozart, Tchaikovsky, and others. A conductor is sure to choose some music from this group of pieces.

There is also much good music that is not heard as often as the standard repertoire. A conductor may wish to include music that is not so familiar in order to give his programs variety.

A constant stream of new music is being written by composers, and the conductor will want to include some of this new music on his programs. Sometimes, he is criticized for having this music played. People complain that they don't understand this new music and that they don't like it.

It is true that "people often don't know what they like, but they like what they know". All of us like familiar things, but as we grow older, we meet new people and new ideas. If you hear a new piece of music, and you don't like it at first, give it another chance —listen again. Think of your best friends. Maybe you didn't like some of them too much at first. A new piece of music is like someone you have just met—you may not like it until you really get to know it.

The time of the year when a concert will be given helps a conductor in choosing music. Handel's *Messiah*, Tchaikovsky's *Nutcracker Suite*, and Bach's *Christmas Oratorio* are heard around Christmas time. It is a tradition that the music from Wagner's *Parsifal* is heard around Easter. The Easter section of the *Messiah* and Rimsky-Korsakoff's *Russian Easter Overture* are also heard near the time of this holiday.

What makes a good concert program? To answer this, let's think about something we're all interested in—a good dinner.

When dad and mother take you out to eat, or when you have a good dinner at home, how does the meal begin? It usually begins with a juice, a soup, or a fruit cup. Something like this increases your appetite and makes you want more. A salad may be placed in front of you next, and then the main course. The idea of the main course is to give you a lot of nourishment. You will probably eat a vegetable and a potato with the meat of the main course. After you have finished the main part of your meal, you will have something sweet—the dessert.

When you stop and think about it, your meal was planned with several ideas in mind. First, there was *variety,* so that you would not get bored. Then it was planned so you would be *interested* in the next thing to appear. It had a point of greatest interest, or a *climax*. To your parents, this may have been a good steak, while you may have found the dessert the most interesting part. When you finished, you were *satisfied*—your hunger was gone, and you were in a good mood.

Suppose we take a look at a concert program to see how it is like a good meal.

Lerner Hall

Cheera Lot Philharmonic Orchestra

Conductor: JOHANN S. TICKWAVING

Overture to La Gazza Ladra..................................Rossini

Mysterious Mountain (Symphony No. 2)...................Hovhaness
    I Andante
   II Moderato maestoso, Allegro vivo
  III Andante espressivo, con moto, molto cantabile,
        andante expressivo

— INTERMISSION —

Concerto No. 5 for Piano and Orchestra in E♭ Major.........Beethoven

Soloist: PLEYITA LONE

  I Allegro
 II Adagio un poco mosso
III Allegro

Rakoczy March...Berlioz

The first number on the program is an overture. This is the kind of overture that is played before an opera. From the opening drum roll to the lively ending, the *Overture to La Gazza Ladra* is quick and sparkling music. It is easy to listen to—the kind of music with which you can quickly become friendly. This piece of music is like the appetizer of a meal. Like a good appetizer, it makes people want more.

The second piece of music, *Mysterious Mountain,* is much different from the first. Like the salad of a meal, it is more filling, and it takes longer than the first number. You will notice that under the name of this music there are Roman numerals. These tell us that there are three *movements,* or parts to this music. After the Roman numerals, you can also see some Italian words. These tell the conductor the tempo, or the speed of the music.

The third selection on the program is the famous *Emperor Concerto* by Beethoven. A concerto (con-CHAIR-tō) is music for solo instrument (one instrument alone) and orchestra. This is the longest number on the program, and contains the most food for thought. To really appreciate this music, you must listen very carefully. As the main course comes just after the middle of a meal, so does the heaviest piece of music come near the middle of a concert.

The final number on the program is the *Rakoczy March* by Berlioz. This is a short, snappy, and stirring march—an ideal ending for this program. As the dessert adds just the right touch to a meal, so does this music finish a concert on the right note. It sends you home in a good mood, which is what the conductor wanted.

Picking Soloists

When a conductor makes out programs, he thinks about the soloists he wants to perform that season. There are several things that he keeps in mind when he chooses solo performers.

First, he tries to have soloists who will draw crowds to the concerts. These are well-known soloists who have pleased audiences for a number of years. Their names are like magic to concert-goers. The conductor knows he will have a full house when these people perform.

Many conductors hire young performers who are not yet well-known to audiences. These are performers who are on the way up. Some will reach the top if they work hard and play well at their concerts. Some conductors feel that they should give chances to gifted young musicians to appear on their programs, and so they are always in search of new talent.

The amount of money in the budget helps the conductor decide just whom he can hire. The younger soloist will not ask as high a fee as the well-known artist. The conductor will probably decide to hire soloists from both groups.

It is important in hiring soloists to think about variety and balance of programs. A conductor will not hire all piano soloists, the same as he will not conduct just symphonies at his concerts. Instead, he will try to hold the interest of his audiences by having soloists on different instruments appear. Sometimes he may choose to have an outstanding singer, or he may want to do a work for chorus and orchestra. This helps to vary the programs.

Whatever he decides, the conductor is careful to have soloists who will keep his audiences interested, and who are fine performers. Soloists add a great deal to the success of the concert season.

Studying Scores

The conductor directs from a *score*. A score is a special part that contains the music for all the instruments. It tells the conductor just what note each player in the orchestra should be playing at any time in the music. When the conductor chose the music for his concerts, he looked at scores to help him pick out the music. When he knows that he will conduct a piece of music in a concert, he studies the score very carefully.

Let's pretend that we are looking over a conductor's shoulder as he studies a score. Most conductors would know the Beethoven fourth symphony, since it is part of the standard repertoire. But if they hadn't conducted it in a while, they would want to go over it again. As we glance over his shoulder, our conductor friend is checking the first movement. Let's see what he is looking at.

25

As our eyes look at the score above, we see that the names of the instruments are listed in front of the music. This is so the conductor will know what notes each instrument should play. The order is always the same. The music for the woodwind instruments is always at the top. The brass parts are always found under the

26

woodwind parts. The timpani and percussion parts are between the brass and the string parts. The string parts are always at the bottom of the score. A conductor grows used to this arrangement, and he always knows just where to look if he has to check a part in a hurry.

As our eyes travel over the score, we see that some of the instruments read from different clefs. Some read music from the treble clef   , some from the alto clef   , and some from the bass clef   . The conductor has to read music in whatever clef he finds.

Those of us who can read music notice something else. We see that the key signature is different for some instruments. The flute, oboe, bassoon, and all the string instruments have a key signature of two flats. The clarinet, horn, and trumpet parts have no sharps or flats.

Instruments are made in several different keys. When the composer writes music, he must choose the correct key for each instrument, so that all the instruments sound right when played together. The conductor must understand the different instruments. He must know, for example, that when the B♭-clarinet plays a B , it is really sounding an A . The composer *transposed* (wrote in a different key) the music for the clarinet to make it sound good with the rest of the instruments.

The timpani part calls for just two notes—B♭ and F. In this case, no key signature is given, but the conductor knows what notes are to be played by looking at the first page of the score. The timpani part looks like this at the beginning.   Timpani in [B♭ / F

Have you noticed the red pencil marks on the score? A conductor marks up a score to remind him of all the important things he must remember while directing the music.

One of the first things some conductors do is to number each measure. Then if a mistake is made, the conductor can call out the exact spot where he wants the orchestra to start.

The dynamic markings are very important to a good performance. They are found on the parts played by the musicians, as well as on the conductor's score. A conductor is sure to mark these. In the example shown, there are six different dynamic markings in thirteen measures. The conductor's pencil has made a note of these.

28

The sign in measure 32, *dim.*, means to get softer, while the *pp* in the next measure means *very softly*. The conductor draws this sign ———————> in with red pencil to remind him of this. It means to get softer, and is easier to see than *dim.* The word in measure 35, *cresc.*, means *louder*, and the *ff* in measure 36 means *very loudly*. The conductor pencils this sign <—————— in measure 35. It means to get louder.

There are two more dynamic marks on these pages. At measure 39 we again notice *ff*, but the word *sempre* is also there. This means to play the music loudly *always*—or until the next sign. The last sign, *fp*, is found in measure 43. This means that the first note is loud and the rest of the notes are soft.

Without these dynamic markings, music would not be nearly as interesting. A good conductor makes sure that the orchestra follows them carefully.

The tempo of the music is also very important. This symphony starts very slowly, but the music changes speed on one of the pages at which we are looking. Do you notice how the conductor has circled the words *Allegro vivace* (vee-VAH-chā)? They mean that the music is to go much faster. He has also written "in 2" to remind him how many beats there are in a measure. The conductor has to be ready for such a spot as this. He must show very clearly how fast the new tempo will be.

A conductor must be sure to bring players in at the right time. If a player starts after the others have been playing, or comes in after a rest, we call the place where he starts to play an *entrance*. The conductor must make sure that the player comes in at the right time. To take care of this, he gives the player a signal, called a *cue*. Helping a player get started at the right time is especially important if there is a solo part for one instrument.

Can you find the timpani part at measure 36? The timpani player has not played a note since the music began. Now he has an important part to play—the music is loud, and the roll of the timpani will add a lot. In addition to adding to the volume, it makes you think something is going to happen. And sure enough, it is—this is just before the tempo change we mentioned earlier. Notice that the conductor has very carefully marked this entrance. He wants to make sure that the player comes in exactly right.

Do you see the *a2* in measure 36? This is to tell two trumpet players to play the same notes. The composer did this to bring out these notes. This was the balance he wanted at this spot. Our conductor will make sure that the balance at this point is what he thinks the composer wanted.

Not every conductor will mark a score in the same way, but most conductors will mark a score when they study it. Now that you have seen some of the many things a conductor must watch, don't you think that marking a score is a good idea?

Rehearsing the Orchestra

After the conductor has studied a score, the next step is to *rehearse,* or practice the music with the orchestra.

There are those who say a conductor should be like a good teacher. A good teacher will try many different ways to help his pupils understand an idea. A good conductor will use many different ways to get the sound he wants. Sometimes he will tell stories. At other times he will shout, or he will whisper. He will even sing to show the players what he wants.

There are two ways in which conductors run their rehearsals. One kind of rehearsing is called the *part method.* Conductors who rehearse this way stop every time something is not exactly right. It seems as though they want to show the musicians what a good ear they have to hear all the mistakes. Such conductors usually insist that rehearsals are run as strictly as concerts. They want results immediately! This type of conductor usually needs a large amount of rehearsal time.

31

The other kind of a rehearsing is called the *whole-part-whole*, or *play-through method.* The conductor who rehearses this way has the orchestra play right through the music at the start. While at a rehearsal, his mind is working in two directions at once. First, he has to inspire the players to find the right mood of the music. Second, he has to listen very carefully to decide where the orchestra is not playing the music exactly as he wishes. Later, he will work on those parts of the music that were not up to his standards. When all the mistakes are corrected, he will probably go through the entire section of music once more, so the players can hear how the whole piece sounds. Can you see how this way of rehearsing got its name?

This type of rehearsing gives the players a chance to be familiar with the music before the conductor demands that it be perfect. The conductor who rehearses this way thinks of a rehearsal as a time for getting ready for a concert, not as a concert. He plans so that there is improvement from one rehearsal to the next. He even expects improvement between the last rehearsal and the concert. While it would seem that this kind of rehearsing needs a lot of time, it usually works out that it needs less time than the part method.

Time is important to both the conductor and the men in the orchestra. The players do not like to see their time wasted. The conductor will know where the hard parts are if he has studied the score. Sometimes, however, mistakes are heard in parts that the conductor did not expect would cause trouble. He must decide quickly which mistakes are "slips" by the players, and which ones are serious enough to need a lot of work.

Before rehearsal, the conductor should have seen that all the parts are correct. If any of the music has been *cut*, or taken out, this must be clearly marked. Some conductors will want the string parts bowed and the breathing spots clearly marked for the wind players. Others will allow the players to decide these matters for themselves.

How Does a Conductor Show the Orchestra How to Play?

The conductor has four ways of giving his ideas to the orchestra. Two of these are easily seen by the audience. One way is seen only by the orchestra. The fourth way is felt by both orchestra and audience.

Let's talk about what the audience and orchestra can see. Both groups watch the hands and the body of the conductor. The attention of most people is drawn to the right, or *time beating hand* of the conductor. This is the hand that holds the baton. Almost all orchestra conductors today use a baton. Sometimes conductors will put the baton down during a piece of music, but usually a conductor looks and acts as though the baton is part of his arm.

Many people think that the conductor just grabs the stick and starts to wave. There are right ways and wrong ways to hold the baton. A good way to hold the baton is shown above.

The position the conductor takes is very important. Have you ever watched a conductor who grew so interested in the music that he leaned over and put his face close to the conductor's stand? This is not a good position to use. Both the audience and the orchestra get the feeling that this kind of conductor is not very sure of himself. Instead, it is a good idea for the conductor to make people feel he is standing very tall and erect in front of the orchestra.

The best position for the hands and arms is right in front of the body. Here is where all beginning, ending, and stopping signals are given.

Some conductors start an orchestra with both hands high over their heads. Others hold both hands way out at the sides.

Sometimes, if a conductor is conducting a very large group made up of many orchestras, choirs, or bands, he may have to make his movements larger. Then he may choose to conduct with his hands high, or his arms out at the sides.

The clearest conductor, however, is the one who holds his arms mostly in front of his body. When the arms move far to the side or higher than usual, the musicians know to look for something important. The conductor whose arms are not in front of his body to begin with, cannot bring out sudden changes in the music as clearly. Musicians say that he does not have a "good beat".

There are special *patterns,* or ways of beating time, that musicians know. All conductors use these patterns a good bit of the time. The four given below will give you an idea of what we mean.

Two beats per measure

 or

Three beats per measure

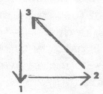 or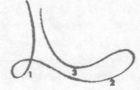

Four beats per measure

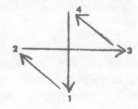 or

Six beats per measure

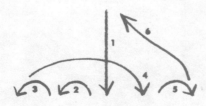 or

35

There are some conductors who stick too closely to these patterns. "But," you say, "how can this be possible? Aren't these patterns the way all music should be conducted?"

Yes, and no. Do you remember the tune our keyboard conductor played earlier? Let's look at it now to show what we mean.

The first measure has four quarter notes. If the conductor follows the pattern for 4/4-time, he clearly beats four notes. In the first measure this is fine, but what about the second measure? There are two quarter notes and a half note in the second measure. If we draw a picture of this rhythm, it looks like this: — — —— , or ♩♩♩ . If the conductor follows the regular pattern, the rhythm he beats will be — — — — , or ♩♩♩♩ . If he makes every beat the same, your friend Jim, who isn't too smart to begin with, may decide to play four equal notes. If Jim doesn't play four quarter notes, he may give just a little push in the middle of the half note —right at the point where the conductor's baton shows the fourth beat. This spoils the music.

The beat-pattern of some good conductors will look like the music sounds. Instead of beating four beats that are exactly the same, they will make the fourth beat much smaller than usual. They make sure that the baton moves so that the players know where the fourth beat is, but the beat is not so strong that Jim wants to give an extra toot! Their pattern for the second measure might look something like this.

There are other times when a conductor will want to change his beat to look like the music sounds. Sometimes the music will sound bouncy, as in the example below. The conductor will make his beats short, so they look like the music. In the second measure, he will lengthen his beat and make it look smoother for the half note.

Conductors who beat time in exactly the same way for every piece of music are called "time-beaters" by musicians. Musicians are not anxious to play for such conductors. A performance by a "time-beater" will not be nearly so exciting as music conducted by someone who feels the music deeply, and shows it in his conducting.

The next time you go to a concert, will you look for some things that are important? Notice that when the music is loud, the conductor makes large movements with his baton. When the music is soft, he makes smaller movements. Watch very closely at the beginning and end of a piece of music. Believe it or not, one of the very hardest things for a conductor to do is to start and stop the orchestra. Good conductors work a long time to get a good start or *attack*, and a good ending, or *release*.

We haven't said anything yet about the conductor's left hand. Does he use it at all? If he does, what does it do? The right hand is used to beat time, while the left hand tells the musicians how to play. The left hand is important in telling the players how loud or soft to play. Another time the left hand is used is when a cue is given. Remember how the conductor marked the timpani entrance in the Beethoven symphony? Well, at such a place he would give a signal, or cue, to the timpani player. He would probably use his left hand to give the cue.

The left hand should not make the same motions as the right hand. One hand beating time is enough. Two are not needed.

Stand in front of a mirror. Now beat the pattern for 3/4-time with the right hand. Remember, the pattern looks like a triangle . Beat three beats with both hands. The left hand "mirrors", or copies the right hand. Now you are making two triangles . This does not help musicians in any way.

Beat 3/4-time again with the right hand. Instead of doing the same thing with the left hand, turn your left palm up, and slowly move your hand up as though you are asking an orchestra to play louder. Continue beating with the right. Now, ask the orchestra to play softer with the left hand. Not as easy as you thought, is it?

So far we've mentioned just two of the ways a conductor tells the orchestra what he wants. The third way is seen only by the orchestra. What might it be?

It has been said that a conductor's eyes control what an orchestra does even more than his baton. Most musicians will agree that how a conductor uses his eyes is important. The eyes can give several cues while the hand is giving only one. The look on a conductor's face can help a great deal, also. A good *conductor looks like the music,* the same as his *beat looks like the music.*

There is one more way that a conductor gives his ideas to the orchestra. This is something that can't be seen—it can only be felt. It is not felt by touching something or someone. Adults would say it is the conductor's "presence".

To explain what we mean, let's think about grown-ups. For some adults, you behave because you have to behave—the adults make you. For other grown-ups you don't behave at all. For still other adults, you behave because you want to. You both like and respect these people. Their "presence" makes you feel that way.

It is the same for conductors. The players will play for some of them because they have to—they want their pay. Some conductors have trouble with orchestras, the same as adults do with young people. Other conductors are both liked and respected by the musicians in an orchestra. They can inspire the orchestra members to do their best.

38

What Makes a Good Conductor?

The story is told of a rich man who wanted to be a conductor. Because he had a lot of money, he hired an entire orchestra and started to rehearse a program. Things didn't go too well. After an hour or so, everyone was quite unhappy. The timpani player got all mixed up because he couldn't follow the man's beat. He soon got about sixteen measures ahead of the rest of the orchestra. In the middle of some very quiet music, he suddenly came in—bang, crash, boom!—with a loud roll. The conductor got mad! He threw down his baton, stared at the orchestra, and yelled, "Now, who did that?"

Imagine a conductor who didn't know the sound of the timpani! This man did not have what a conductor needs most of all—training and experience. What should we expect of a conductor?

First of all, the conductor must be a good musician. He usually plays some instrument very well, and he has probably studied several other instruments. He must know just what each instrument in the orchestra can do. A conductor usually knows quite a lot about *composition,* or composing music, and about *orchestration,* the art of writing music for the different instruments in the orchestra. If he has studied orchestration, he understands how to transpose music, and he knows the different clefs that are used. From playing in an orchestra and from studying an instrument, he has learned the Italian musical terms. Also, during his orchestra experience, he has learned the repertoire. He has a good ear and a good sense of rhythm.

The conductor must know how to work with people. He must be a good leader whom others can respect and trust. He must be able to take a group of musicians and make them into an orchestra.

He should be a good teacher. There are times when he has to be very patient. He must be able to explain things so that the members of the orchestra understand what he wants.

He should be a good *interpreter.* This means that he can take the music of another man, the composer, and conduct the orchestra in such a way that the other man's musical ideas are clearly heard. No two conductors can make an orchestra or a piece of music sound the same. Some of each personality will come through in the music. But the composer's ideas are the most important, and the conductor should not change them.

The conductor is like the coach of a football team, and he is like the quarterback, too. He picks a style of play, the music; he drills the players, the rehearsal; and he calls the signals, the concert.

How do we judge how good a conductor is? By two things: how good his musical thoughts are, and how complete his control is over his musical instrument—the orchestra.

Is a Conductor Necessary?

Is a conductor necessary? You have just finished reading about some of the many things a conductor does. Can these things be done without some one person to do them? A car will go without a driver. Would you want to ride in it? An orchestra can play without a conductor. Would you want to listen to it, or would you want to play in it?

You decide.

ABOUT THE AUTHOR

Robert W. Surplus, a native of Gouldsboro, Pennsylvania, has been active in music education almost twenty years. He has had experience in every phase of music education in the public schools, and has taught all age levels from kindergarten through graduate school. Formerly Supervisor of Music at Red Lion, Pennsylvania, Associate Professor at Shippensburg State College, Shippensburg, Pennsylvania, and Instructor at Teachers College, Columbia University, he is at present, an Assistant Professor in the College of Education, University of Minnesota. A graduate of Susquehanna University with a Bachelor of Science degree, and of Teachers College, Columbia with a Master of Arts degree, he is presently completing the requirements for a doctorate at Columbia University.

We specialize in publishing quality books for
young people. For a complete list please write

LERNER PUBLICATIONS COMPANY

133 First Avenue North, Minneapolis, Minnesota 55401